Publisher
Marolyn D. Evans
P.O. Box 18233
Pensacola, Florida 32532-8233

Cover Design

Linda C-Holliday
Angel78productions

Graphic
Yellow Bird Graphics

Story Editor/Editor
Linda C-Holliday

First Printing March 2019
ISBN: 13 - 978-1-7327766-2-3

WHO AM I

A Memoir

Written by

Debbie Staples

Dedication

In Loving Memory

To my beloved Angels, This book
is dedicated to the memories of
my two late grandsons,

Jerome and Micah.

I relish the glorious kingdom of
God where your precious spirits
dwells. My love for you both is
forever resting in your
grandmother's heart.
Missing you greatly! We will
always love you! Your sweet
loving memories will live on in
all of your family's hearts
forever! Our love for you both, is
Great!

But, God loves you best!

Table of Contents

About the Author

Acknowledgements

Thanks! To my glorious Lord and Savior Jesus Christ, without Him I would not be **Who I Am** today.

To my loving husband Collin, what a blessing you've been in my life. The great King of Wisdom scribed this powerful passage of love between a man and his wife... Whoso findeth a wife findeth a good thing, and obtaineth favour of the LORD. With that special favor from our creator you transcend life and love with me. Collin, I thank God daily for blessing me with a husband who loves the Lord 1st with all of his heart. Honey, you are truly a man after God's own heart! You've always inspired me to believe in myself, and the gifts that God has given me. I'm so honored to be your wife and your best friend! My prayer is that we continue to walk in oneness before God and His people. I love you my husband, so very much, thanks for supporting me and my endeavors! God Bless You, Man of God!

I give honor to my loving parents; my beautiful mother Mrs. Molly Johnson and my father Mr. Julius Myricks; you've loved me beyond measure. You have both given me the holy foundation of God's word to direct me for a lifetime. You are both loved. My heart and soul attends to you both, continuously. May God continue to bless you!

Apostle Dr. Linda Holliday you are my Angel sent from God overflowing with his Holy Spirit and his Love. When you came into my life, God's Glory manifested through many countless acts of kindness. There have been trials, and storms along the way, but you have shown me what to do and how to pray. When I felt like giving up, your words of wisdom lifting me up. When I experience days of pain and despair, you were always there to show you care. When I felt so all alone you reminded that God's love is strong. When I couldn't cope with life's challenges, you let me know in God there is Hope. Because of you and all your love, I know that God sent you from above. I love you Apostle Holliday.

Bishop Williams Reynolds, your voice echoes constantly the scripture of God's plans for me in... *Jeremiah 29:11 "For I know the plans I have for you" declares the Lord, plans to prosper you and not to harm you, plans to give you hope and a future.* The Lord knew just who to anchor as a pillar in my life, guiding me along my life's journey, encouraging me to fulfill the purpose and destiny God has for me. Thanks so much for being the willing vessels used by God to change my life.

Laura, thanks for all the years of love, wisdom and encouragement. You are so appreciated and I want you to know that I love you so much.

Moses, what can I say to a person who always has a joke to share whenever I was going through? Thanks so much Moses for being who God has called you to be in this family.

To my sisters Michelle, and Deeneen, you two have been voices of inspiration in my life. Thank you both for always giving sound advice regarding my children. Thanks for all your support, encouragement, and love.

 To my brother Todd, what a wonderful brother you are; always giving advice and support whenever I needed you. I love you Todd.

To my amazing children, Kimberly, Telia, Mia, Tiffany and Tyrone, there aren't enough words to express my love for you and your accomplishments in life. Your love, challenges, trials, tribulations, defeats and celebrations have truly inspired me to discover **Who I Am** as a mother and grandmother. Because of all of you I've been able to face the most difficult decisions in my life. I want you all to know that you have been the motivating force behind my perseverance and tenacity. Accordingly, you are the reason that I have never once even though of giving up no matter how difficult or challenging things may have been for us. Thank you all for being *"the wind beneath my wings."* I am so proud of you all and I love each of you unconditionally!

To my grandchildren, Jamyia, Derraya, Desharay, Jaylen, Titus, Tahara, Karter, Best Friend (A.K.A.) Jacob, Jeremiah, Jerome, Micah, Kelly, Jada, Emily, Dacklan, Ethan, Ajuwauhn, Jaylen, Kassidy, Khaliagh, Jordon, Jalen, Zyan, Raegyn, Harli, Gavin, and Landon, I love you all so very much! Always remember to "BELIEVE" in your dreams and goals and know that I'm always your biggest cheerleader in whatever you do! I love you all!

Special Thanks

Hair Stylist:
Tamika (Tiki) Baytops
Your hair designs accelerates the beauty of
God in me
Thank you for every one of our weekly chats

To my Weaver family,
I've been blessed to be able to be reunited
with all of you

My Alabama family,
Once again. Thank you all for loving and
accepting me!

Family and friends:
My prayer is that you all will know that I
count it an honor and I feel enormously
blessed to have you in my life! Your
conversations, prayers, and words of
wisdom will never be forgotten as I continue
this journey on the road to discovering
"Who I Am in God".

To Jovon
What a prized treasure you are from God!
I thank God for you and
I love you so very much!

Preface

To all of you my valued readers – As you read this book and reflect back over your past, present, and future life, I pray that you will *become* liberated, delivered and set free from your past hurts and pains that has held you captive. Moreover, I pray that you will embrace the unique, talents, and gifts God has ordained you with. *God created you for His purpose! Hence, you were created in the likeness and image of God!*

As you begin to ask yourself the question **"Who Am I"**? I pray that you will discover truth and beauty within YOU! In addition, it is my sincere prayer and my heart's desire that you will find inner peace, joy, love, and happiness as you begin this journey of loving and nurturing the new YOU! Embrace the beautiful human that God has called and destined you to *be!*

Upon completion of reading this book you will see, you're no longer bound by the circumstances and disappointments of your past! No more burdens or strongholds chained to your destiny. You've obtained divine revelation and restoration through the blood of the sacrificial Lamb of God! Rest in the Lord and wait patiently for Him!

Finally, beloved, I pray that my book **Who Am I** will encourage your heart, inspire your soul, and motivate you to embrace your true identify as you begin to believe the report of the Lord. Ask yourself Who Am I? your internal response will say *...I am strong, talented, valued, intelligent, unique, gifted, beautiful, amazing, smart, a child of the Most High God, More than a*

15

conqueror, an overcomer with a purpose driven life. I am God's son or daughter, I am an heir of salvation and a joint heir with Christ. I am God's chosen vessel. I'm the apple of His eye! Therefore, my beloved, I submit to you these words of encouragement; no matter what circumstances or situations that you may face in life, rest assured that God is with you and He will take care of you. You do not have to face life's challenges alone because God has promised to never leave nor forsake you! God loves YOU!

Introduction

I cried, and cried out to the Lord time after time after time… LORD I NEED YOU!! LORD I NEED YOU!! There was confusion and heartaches, shame, and brokenness. The wind storms came with rolls of thunder. There were tears and more tears and my lord heard that cry and ministered to me out of His word from the book of Isaiah. He gave me hope speaking in chapter 54 by saying I am your creator, your husbandman…*Fear not; for thou shalt not be ashamed: neither be thou confounded; for thou shalt not be put to shame: for thou shalt forget the shame of thy youth, and shalt not remember the reproach of thy widowhood any more. For thy Maker is thine husband; the Lord of hosts is his name; and thy Redeemer the Holy One of Israel; The God of the whole earth shall he be called. For the LORD hath called thee as a woman forsaken and grieved in spirit, and a wife of youth, when thou wast refused, saith thy God. For a small moment have I forsaken thee; but with great mercies will I gather thee. In a little wrath I hid my face from thee for a moment; but with everlasting kindness will I have mercy on thee, saith the LORD thy Redeemer.*

From that moment of love and redemption I came into the knowledge of **"Who I Am"**! So in my daily devotion I give honor to my Lord and Savior Jesus Christ.

I 've been encouraged several times that I'm holding a book of inspiration in my womb that will release, deliver, set free, restore faith, and hope in the lives of God's people. I present to you an account of my life's journey. This book will not only minister to those individuals who find themselves standing in the need for restoration as I did, but it will also minister to those who struggle with identity issues not knowing who you really are.

Lord God... I am eternally grateful and appreciative to You because You have allowed me to release my pain, share my experiences and embrace the most tragic moments of my life with Your Spirit of healing! Lord, you have taken away my fears of the unknown that has kept my mind in captivity with you. Father, Your Holy Spirit has unlocked the chambers of my mind, soul, and spirit and now I am better able to minister to the world being a blessing to your people.

Who Am I? Seemingly, this very important question has stirred the minds of every generations of people from all around the world, from many cultures, ethnicities, and gender. Perhaps, you've asked yourself that very same question **Who Am I?** And what's my purpose in life? You may be on a quest to determine your purpose in life and questioned why were you born? Could the truth of the matter possibly be as simple as the fact that you were created by God for His good pleasure and glory? Could it be that you were created with a divine purpose and plan in mind? Could it be that you were created to make His praise glorious?

As I share my personal life experiences in this book, including my challenges, trial, tribulations, hurts, pain, shame, and disappointments, dreams, blessings, accomplishments, and the revelations regarding **Who I Am**, who I once was, and the person I am becoming, I pray that you will be inspired and motivated to become the person that God has created you to be. In addition, it is my heart's desire that you will find inner peace as you begin the journey of loving who you are and the person God has created you to become.

Embrace the journey and enjoy the ride!

Chapter 1

People See... Who I Am

As I began to take an inventory of my life I look back reflecting on what my life was over the years. Even at this stage of maturity I continuously asked myself at times "Who Am I"? And when I asked God the same question, then He reveals to me that *I am somebody special, created for His glory!* God assures me that I am valued, I am loved, and I am a child of the Most High God.

Jesus Himself had an encounter with His disciples conversa ting that some of the people knew He was the Christ but others question who He was... *And Jesus went out, and his disciples into the towns of Caesarea Phillippi: and by the way He*

asked His disciples, saying unto them,
Whom do men say that I am? And they
answered, John the Baptist; but some say,
Elias; and others, One of the prophets. And
He saith unto them, but whom say ye that I
am? And Peter answereth and saith unto
Him, Thou art the Christ.   Mark 8:27-29.

Jesus knew who He was: the holy one of God the messiah but he wanted to know who His People perceived him to be; was He really somebody special a great king the Master, the alpha and omega.

I am thankful to God he has made me a light unto His people for all to see. I often hear of people telling me that I am somebody. Even my children, friends, and church family tells me that I'm somebody, but, what's most interesting is that my family members tells me that I'm not just "somebody" but I am "everybody" . They say that with my kindness and gentleness I become everything to everybody; helping to meet their needs.

I marvel and find it interesting how their perception of me does not change while in fact I am yet continuously evolving in to all God has appointed me to be for Him and His saints. I am constantly asking myself **who am I**? Although I wear many hats as I serve the different needs of the people of God, my talents are gifted from God to love, and be a blessing to uplift the family of God. God uses me from talent to talent just as a chameleon changes into its many hues of colors and fits right into its environment going unnoticed; so does God use me with many attribute and colorful characteristics of the Lord's transforming powers as he used me.

"Who Am I?" And what's the beauty behind knowing who I am as a woman and a child of God? As I awake each morning, I persistently pondered with the thoughts of who will I be on that particular day. Imagine with me my thoughts, in agony, and frustration that I felt each day. The uncertainty of not knowing or being clear who I am or better yet, not having the slightest idea of what others, may think of me. The acceptance of my family, friends, spouse, church, students, colleagues and most importantly, my Lord and Savior, was of importance to me. What did I have to do to please them all? What would I need to supply the needs of who would call me that day? Will I please God today or would I disappoint Him. Well, it would just razzle my soul, I would feel weak and simply walked in fear and devastation throughout the day. It has taken many years of self-searching and asking myself this question "Who Am I? I eventually came to the realization of Who I Am and now I have come to an understanding that *I'm someone that has a unique gift and purpose in life!* I am destined for God's greatness in life! If you are a child of God then you, too, are destined for greatness! Understand that in order to tap into that greatness, you must *allow your mind to enter into a place of divine discovery and acceptance!*

I would like to share an amazing experience with you. One day when I was at home in a very quiet atmosphere, I begin to listen to what the Holy Spirit was speaking to me. As my feet stood motionless at the side of my bed, I began to hear the Holy Spirit speak clearly…

"Debbie, I need for you to be a servant to people of higher authority over you. I need for you to be the sustainer of hope and faith to my people who are struggling in their faith. I need for you to provide spiritual guidance and counsel to individuals that may be experiencing emotional challenges in life."

Moreover, the Lord is speaking to me as I clearly hear Him saying *"Debbie my servant, your pain and suffering was not in vain. They are no longer a hindrance in your life or your ministry. I, the Lord, have chosen you to be great among men. Debbie, understand that in the spiritual realm I've birth in you and will soon birth out of you a host of blessings to many generations. Eye hath not seen, nor ear heard, neither have entered into the heart of man, the things which God hath prepared for them that love him. 1 Corinthians 2:9.*

This birth will be a mystery to mankind but a blessing to God! You, Debbie, must realize that questions will be surfacing your mind, but trust Me for the answers as you continue to listen to the voice of the Holy Spirit and embrace your God given gifts, talents, and abilities.

While I continue to ask "Lord, Who Am I?" "Who Am I, my Lord?" "Who Am I?" The question continues to captivate my spirit. One quiet day as I was sitting at home, I heard the Holy Spirit whispering these profound words to my inner soul ***"Debbie, no one will ever know who You Are until you acknowledge who I have called you to be!"*** *I could hear God say to me that He has* blessed me with unimaginable gifts and talents among men.

Perhaps, some of you may be much like I was and unaware of the gifting's that God has placed inside of you. If that's the case then I encourage you to allow the Holy Spirit to speak to you. I submit to you this day that there are many gifts and talents stored on the inside of you.

Subsequently, some of you may be experiencing thoughts of unworthiness, unimportance, feelings of inadequacy, insignificance or even thoughts that your life doesn't matter. Remember, those thoughts are false, they are tricks from the enemy. The truth is that you are important and your life does matter. You matter to God and you matter to the people that love you. You are significant, and you are valued in the Kingdom of God!

Allow me to share with you my past thoughts of inadequacy and the many years of torment, and anguish that I endured in my soul. The Holy Spirit began to speak the truth of my existence through dreams, and visions. The truth is that one day, unexpectedly, God revealed the truth to me as I was sitting at home minding my own business and reflecting back over my life. I will, indeed, share this revelation and more with you in greater details as you continue to read through the remaining chapters of this book.

The vision that God revealed to me was plain and clear. God said "Debbie, as you continue to see the illusions of life and death, I will continue to show you where the supernatural divine power rests in the cavities of your soul. You continue to ask yourself the question "Who Am I." *I will soon reveal the truth to you!"*

Many Christians in addition to non-Christians often ask themselves the question "Who is God?" Is God real?" Some People have even questioned if Christ has ever walked upon the face of the Earth. And the questions lingers: Can God heal the sick? Can God cause the blind to see? Did God really raise Lazarus from the Dead? Did God heal the woman with the issue of blood?

Even though people still doubt Who God Is. It's no secret to those that believe in Him. God is God and besides Him there is no other. God is mighty. God is powerful. God is loving. God is Kind. He's ever merciful and He's forgiving. God is sovereign, He's omniscient meaning infinite knowledge, omnipotent meaning unlimited power and omnipresent meaning present everywhere. God loves you and He cares about you. God knows your name and He knows every hair on your head.

One day, the Holy Spirit revealed something quite amazing to me regarding my demeanor of humbleness during times of adversity, agony and pain that has often occupied my mind and left me feeling defeated in the natural, yet, strong in the spiritual realm. The Holy Spirit revealed to me that I am a child of the most High God. He revealed to me that I am a woman with a "divine" *purpose of destiny*. He revealed that I have strength beyond imagination. He spoke to me saying "Debbie, you see the unseen as a result of your willingness to believe in illusions, visions, and images that seem to plague your mind of curiosity."

Your heart's desire is to satisfy your soul with glorifying Me, that's priceless and speaks volumes! "Yes, My beloved daughter, *you are Somebody*"!

As I continue to cry out to the Lord Who Am I? The Holy Spirit continues to speak loudly to me and instructs me to continue to search and cry out for answers to Who I Am. The Holy Spirit instructed me to have faith and believe that one day the answers will be revealed to me.

The Holy Spirit spoke these words to me "My beloved child, you should think of the wind that sways in various directions. You, too, will sway in many directions that I have chosen for you, but, be not dismayed nor discouraged because I am with you always and you can depend on Me. I am your God and besides Me there is no other God".

As the *Holy Spirit ministered to me, my heart began to heal.* "Yes, Debbie, you cried, you cried often my beloved daughter but it was all in God's plan. Just as I endured much suffering for mankind. I endured excruciating pain, persecution, fear, rejection, emotional and physical beatings beyond recognition on the Cross of Calvary. I did it all for you and for mankind. I endured the Cross because I love you! I became sin, even though I knew no sin so that you might become the righteousness of God in Christ Jesus!"
"My child I love you dearly!"

"I was nailed to the Cross and pierced in the side. Yes, I endured the pain, but it was all for

My good and it was for God's glory! It was all in God's ultimate plan for humanity."

Once again the Holy Spirit began speaking to me with a loud voice calling out "Debbie, my beloved daughter, do not cease to believe that your persecutions have not been in vain. I have felt your pain and I am your comforter," says the Lord.

The Holy Spirit continued to speak to me for many years and eventually I began to embrace the vision and walk in the calling that God has purposed for my life. Have you ever wondered if you are walking in your God given purpose?

I will share with you the exact scripture in the book of Job that the Holy Spirit revealed to me during my time of uncertainty and doubt. The Holy Spirit instructed me to read

Job 29:11 *"For I know the thoughts that I think toward you, saith the LORD, thoughts of peace, and not of evil, to give you an expected end."* For I have seen and heard your cry, Debbie. I see you going back and forth, back and forth in your mind asking and wondering "When will my deliverance come? When will my release come? When will my change come? When will the pain, torment and sadness go away?" I, the Lord your God is saying "Conquer the un-clean Spirits with the Spirit of the living God."

The Holy Spirit whispered these words to me "Debbie, your strength lies in Me, your God. Remember, the words that I revealed to you earlier today, *"Rest in Me."* Yes, I want you to **Rest in Me,** my beloved daughter! Your mind should be filled with thoughts of Me, your soul's desire should be to please Me and your ultimate reason for living should be to allow My will for your life be done.

Debbie, who will you be on tomorrow? I reluctantly answered, I don't know, I'm not exactly sure who I will be on tomorrow. I guess the answer depends on who needs me most on tomorrow and who they will need me to be. My child, you must continue to keep your hands to the plow, and trust in Me with all your heart to guide you with wisdom and knowledge."

As you continue to read this book, I would like to share with you that the Holy Spirit hasn't left me alone a single day without ministering to my feelings of brokenness and moments of disbelief. Understand, that God wanted us as Christians to stop doubting the power and greatness that He has instilled in each one of us through His Holy Spirit. I believe that one day, soon and very soon, I will rise above the doubt and uncertainly and I will no longer wonder or question Who I Am.

There were even times that I've pondered in my mind who do I represent in terms of biblical characters in the Bible. Which woman of God do I portray in my past, present and future life? I have questioned "Am I even deserving enough to entertain such thoughts in my mind? Can I compare myself or better yet even measure up to a biblical character or a biblical women of God?"

As I began to speak the words and tell myself yes, of course, I have the right and I do measure up based on the finished works of the Cross. Jesus died for my sins and He took all of my mistakes, shame, and guilt on the Cross with Him. I am redeemed by the blood of the Lamb and the Word of my testimony. I know now for sure that I am Somebody. I am special and loved in the sight of God.

However, there are still moments that I find myself comparing me, Debbie, to everyone else. I often compare myself to other mothers, wives, women of God, professional women, women of beauty, women with financial status, educated women etc. I realize that God made me to be the best me and I'm striving each day to become what God has called me to be. I am a work-in-progress and one day I will get my crown!

I have often ask and wondered, when will the cycle end. I have come to realize that the spinning cycle ends once I take the initiative to start believing In me, the what?

And the who? God- says that I am. I understand now that I should have only compared myself to the image of my Lord and Savior because He is my Heavenly Father and He created me in His image. I know now that my Heavenly Father gave me an abundant life designed for His purpose and plan. Prior to the Holy Spirit revealing my divine purpose to me, I never really understood why I was born or who I was as a child of God.

The questions in my mind usually included such questions as: Who Am I God, Why Do you keep on allowing me to live? What is best for me? Where do you want me to go? What do you want me to do? Will my past experiences and choices hinder me from doing your will? Am I worthy of the call on my life? Will my gifts bring glory and honor to your name? I would often tell God that I've made so many past mistakes in life and that I can't imagine myself being valuable to the Kingdom of God.

More often than not it appeared as though my mind was tormented with thoughts of defeat and failure. I compared myself at the time to a fish that was caught on a hook and the line was constantly shaking and twisting. Much like a captured fish, I couldn't get released or escape from my state of captivity. In regards to the fish analogy, eventually a fish, after being captured, gives up the fight mainly due to the fact that there are no more fight or life lines left. Hence, he is not only captured but defeated. In his state of defeat, a captured fish will just lay there motionless until the fisherman would release him from the hook. Unlike the captured, motionless, and defeated fish, I refuse to give up and throw in the towel. I refuse to lay down and give up my life like a fish. I was determined to persevere. You see, I had been through too much in my life, the devil had tormented me too many times, and the enemy had captured my mind with lies too often for me to give up now. I soon realized that through prayer, perseverance, and the aide of the Holy Spirit, I was able to stand firm on the Word of God. I eventually gained strength and power to resist and rebuke the lies, deception, and deceit of the devil. I came to the realization that only God has complete and total power and control over my mind. Understand, that we can't allow the enemy to take control of our emotions and thoughts. We must allow the mind of Christ to resonate and be in us at all times. The ultimate power and control of our mind and thoughts reside in the power of God. *Thou wilt keep him in perfect peace, whose mind is stayed on thee: because He trusteth in thee. Isaiah 26:3.* Also, in the book of 2nd Timothy Chapter 1 Verse 7: the writer reminds us that; *God has not given us the spirit of fear; but of power and of love and of a sound mind. Amen*!

Chapter 2

The Loss of My Grandson

Jerome Moore

*And He said unto me, My Grace is
sufficient for thee: for my strength is made
perfect in weakness.*

2 Corinthians 12:9

In this chapter, I will share with you some of
my traumatic experiences coupled with my
emotional highs and lows. Consequently,
there was a time in my life, around the year
of 2007, when one of my daughters lost her
baby son. This was a time in my life when I
was truly devastated and deeply sadden in
my heart. One day in the midst of it all, I
heard the voice of God instructing me to
keep on praising him no matter what the
cost, no matter what happened. Remarkably,

during that same time, I was also blessed with an indescribable visitation from the Holy Spirit.

Notably, I recall one day as I was sitting in a church service, I began praising God with great passion. I began crying out to God and giving Him thanks for His grace and mercy toward me and my family. I knew at that moment that God was the most important person or being in my life and that I truly loved the Lord with all of my heart, soul, mind, and spirit.

Allow me to pause and back up for just a minute...You see, in previous weeks just prior to my attending this particular church service, time was spent ministering to family, friends, and coworkers, sharing with them my genuine love for God and how I trusted God with my life. I distinctly recall, telling God how much I appreciate and thanked Him for blessing me with such a wonderful family and loving husband who embraced me during my many shortcomings, failures, and disappointments and still reserves a place in his heart to love me unconditionally. I admit, I'm a truly blessed woman! Praise The Lord! I put this question before you...have you ever experienced such deep level of appreciation for all the wonderful things that God has allowed to happen in your life? Of course, you can relate to my overwhelming feelings of gratitude! However, during that same period of time, I also recall rebuking the devil and telling him that there is nothing that he could ever say or do to me that would cause me to reject my God and lose my joy. My faith, love and commitment toward God is steadfast and unwavering.

During this specific time in my life, I had not yet experienced speaking in tongues, referred to by many Christians as speaking in a "Heavenly Language." I would like to tell you just for the record that day was very special to me. It all started with my husband and I being invited to a concert at a Church. I remember seeing one of my favorite Christian recording artist there. I recall telling my husband how extremely excited I felt in my spirit. For some unknown reason, I just couldn't cease from giving God the highest praise during the service. Immediately, upon our arrival at the church, I could feel the presence of God in the atmosphere as we stepped foot on the ground. Once we entered the church, the

Spirit was even higher and I found myself standing, and praising God for almost the entire service. In other words, I just couldn't get off my feet. I couldn't stop praising and worshipping my God!

This particular concerts was one of the best praise and worship experiences I have ever encountered in life. I praised God relentlessly for His greatness, His love and His acceptance of me. I praised and thanked God for not allowing me to experience a life of sadness any more. I praised him for His Word and for blessing me with a husband that no one would ever believe or think that I could have. I realize that God did it just for me and I am truly thankful to God for His goodness toward me. I will share with you greater details about my loving relationship with my husband in the later chapters of this book.

As hours past and the evening grew late, I discovered a boldness in my Spirit that had overtaken me. I was embolden, and began to speak to the enemy (Satan) and I began to tell him all the things that had been on my heart. I told him that I didn't care about what he wanted to do to me because no matter what, I was still going to trust and serve the Lord until I die. In the past, I have experienced many trials and tribulations after boldly speaking those words but this time, I stood firm, steadfast, and unmovable as I start believing and declaring the promises of our Lord and Savior Jesus Christ.

and I experienced one of the most devastating tragedies one could ever expect. I recall being awaken very early on this particular morning to a phone call. On the other end of the line there was a screeching sound of crying, screaming and a desperate plea of help from my daughter. She was pleading for me to help her as she cried out to me with these words…"Mom he's not moving! Mom he won't wake up! Mom please help me!" I began to cry out in disbelief with her and proceeded to comfort her in my motherly way, and told her that I was on my way, accompanied by my husband. In that moment I felt confusion, devastation and hurt as we drove to her apartment that early morning. When we finally arrived at her apartment, my daughter was just standing there in the apartment embracing her baby and my grandson Jerome in her arms crying uncontrollably and shaking with fear. As I moved in closer to my grandson, my husband began consoling my daughter. The piercing sound of the fire department EMT's played and played over and over far in the back of my mind thinking how surreal this moment was. Soon I began to hear the ambulance sirens closely approaching my daughter's apartment, my heart felt as though it had stopped beating. I had now sunken into deep despair of the happening event.

I recall sitting there feeling helpless, hopeless and hurt as I watched the paramedics try to revive my little grandson Jerome. After several unsuccessful attempts to revive his lifeless body, he was then placed in the ambulance.

We all followed the ambulance to the hospital as we were in a state of shock and disbelief fearing the final outcome of hearing those words, He Is Dead. Once we arrived at the hospital, we were told that Jerome had passed away. Of course, this was the worse news that we had ever expected to receive. Needless to say, this was one of the hardest if not the most difficult day of all our lives. Imagine losing a loving baby and grandbaby in a split of a second. My heart was devastated, the pain wouldn't leave, my spirit, soul, and mind was at a place of depression and my faith wavered. At that moment I did not understand God's plan because now, Jerome, my beautiful grandson was really gone and there was absolutely nothing that I could do about it. The only thing that I could do at that time was cry and hold my daughter in my arms during this very traumatic time of loss of her baby boy.

Well, who was I on that day? I honestly didn't know who I was on that day. Of course, I knew God, but I couldn't understand what was going on or why.

Have you ever found yourself questioning your faith? That's exactly what happened to me I am a living witness and want to encourage you today and let you know that God will heal your broken heart. He absorbed my weakness, as I began to faint he kept me from falling He bored my hurt and comforted me. God will take care of you as he cared for me; no matter what situations or circumstances that you may be facing in life. Just know that *God is with you. The* scriptures remind us that God will heal our broken heart. I am a living witness that the Lord will take care of His own.

I talked to the Lord and I told him that I have had some very unbelievable, difficult days and that almost every day seemed to be a struggle. I recall many weeks of despair. I couldn't find comfort, peace or rest in my soul after losing my grandson. The unimaginable pain that was so deep rooted in my heart seemed like a persistent ache. I recall asking the Lord if the pain would ever end. Frankly, there were some days that I found myself floating into delusions and drifting into a sea of sadness feeling incapable of swimming back to shore or rather a safe place of refuge in the Lord. During this very difficult time in my life, I knew that I needed to write, therefore, I journaled my thoughts of what the Holy Spirit was revealing to me.

My life continued to unravel much like a ball of yarn as I was dealing with and trying to understand the loss of my grandson. Staying close to and being in God's presence was all that I could do. I had never experienced such pain. I realized that God was my only source of my help and strength. He was the sustainer of my mind, soul, and heart. I often asked God these two questions "how long will the pain last and how long will I continue to have sleepless nights?

The tormenting thoughts haunted me as I frequently asked myself what I could have done differently in order to prevent my grandson's death. Theoretically, this question may haunt me for the rest of my life, however, I have found solace in knowing that God is with me. Additionally, I find comfort in meditating and listening to worship music. As of today, I no longer suffer with such overwhelming feelings of sadness.

As I continued to listen to the Lord, I respond "Lord I hear your sweet voice reminding me that you are still here for me even during this darkest hour of my life. Lord, you are my light and my heart will stop hurting because you have healed me. You sent Your Word to heal us! You are healing me right now. You are doing a great work in me and I Thank You, Heavenly Father for blessing me right now!

After several weeks of waiting in anticipation, my grandson's autopsy results eventually arrived. As I begin to open the envelope, I remembered asking God for strength and grace as we read the results of the cause of baby Jerome's death. "Lord, what am I hoping for? What exactly was I wanting to know? However, the very answers that I searched for were not there. Furthermore, there were still so many unanswered questions surrounding his death. I proceeded to read the report only to discover that the document stated "natural causes," but what exactly are "natural causes" I begin to ask myself. What are "natural causes?" I was confused beyond imagination. Have you ever experienced a similar situation and you found yourself questioning God in regards to a situation that made absolutely no "earthly" sense at all? With all that being said, my strong faith in God assured me that my God is a healer and He is the deliverer of my soul. I made up in my mind that I will trust in the Lord like never before. *Who Am I, God? Could it be that I am the pillar of strength that my daughter needed during that time of saddens and great loss in her life?* As time goes on, I do not cease to give God thanks for all that He has done in our lives. I remain steadfast in God's presence as I experience the manifestation of His power and strength in me and through me. Finally, after many years of hurt, pain, and grieving, I begin to trust and believe God for healing and understanding. My heart continued to heal and my loving grandson, Jerome, remains in our hearts; he will never be forgotten. Jerome was only eight months old when he transitioned from this side of Earth to Heaven. In spite of his very young age, Jerome has touched our lives in unimaginable, conceivable ways.

We have experienced the greatest love in knowing him. Our lives will never be the same because of the beauty and joy that he brought! So, Who Am I? I am a grandmother! A grandmother that has been touched by an angel! A grandmother that has been healed from much pain grief and suffering. *Who Am I? I am Grandma Debbie! I am honey! I am best friend! I am Nanna! To all my grandchildren.*

Chapter 3

Consequence of My Choices

If any of you lack wisdom, let him ask of God, that giveth to all men liberally, and upbraideth not; and it shall be given him.
James 1:15

Countless times in my life, I have wondered if my past mistakes and choices in life will help or hinder my spiritual walk with God. I deliberately used the term "past mistakes" lightly because the Lord only knows all that we go through, and Lord knows…I've made my share of mistakes! I have often been terrified and tormented in dreams concerning my failures due to choices in my past. As a very young child I made personal choices with approval or disapproval of my parents. They were the overseers of my life and I was held accountable by them. I respected them and their opinions and at that time I made wiser choices knowing that would please them. My parents always nurtured and cared for me deeply. They protected me and kept me safe. They loved me unconditionally and instilled the love of God in all their children.

We attended Sunday morning worship service regularly every week. If that wasn't enough, we were all very active in the ministry. At times, we were even allowed to choose our own church ministries to participate in and be a part of. I served on the junior usher board in addition to singing in the choir. I recall attending choir rehearsal every Tuesday night at 6:00 p.m. and this is where the pivotal point of my making wrong choices began. I was only 13-14 years old at the time.

Here's how it all began. One day I meet an older guy that found me attractive and told me that I was beautiful. Those were sweet words to my ear. Soon thereafter, I experienced feelings of acceptance from this young guy and I began to feel   self-worth and valued; something that I had not previous felt. This guy had a way to make me feel important and worthy of his attention. And for the first time in my young life, I actually thought for a moment that I was special and that I was somebody. Now, imagine a little skinny looking like the twin to twiggy, almost bald headed comparing my head to a Georgia peach, thick lips that covered the lower half of my face but in the heat of that moment I was a girl being made to feel beautiful. I recall feeling that my smile never mattered to anyone and that it definitely didn't light up a room. Prior to meeting this guy, I felt that I had no real reason to believe in myself. I always devalued myself having this inferiority complex I just didn't think too much of myself. I was yoked to those memes, never seeing the glorious beauty on my face, God had designed in me for His Joy and Pleasure.

Soon, everything begin to change and I actually started believing that this guy really liked and wanted me. I begin to contemplate in my girlish mind that we would someday get marry. Can you imagine that? Me married!

Suddenly, the pain of feeling rejected and unworthy of love creeps in and it is enormously painful. I can recall a time when this guy was always saying the nicest and kindest words to me, he even bought me extremely nice gifts. Needless to say, this young man made me feel like Cinderella in a fairy tale. He was my knight in shining armor, the prince who place the sparkling pump, left behind at the ball that would only fit my foot.

I would often ask Jesus if this guy was truly the one for me, was he my soul mate. Honestly, I began to feel the security in the attention he gave me, and the pain, hurt and rejection slowly began leaving my heart. I must have been thinking that this guy really cared about me with my all my beauty faults and ugliness as I had perceived myself to be at that time. What an amazing feeling as a teenage girl. Obedience was sucked out and all thoughts of being a good girl vanished and I am held in captivity of my flesh, even if it meant disobeying my parent's rules. In my finite mind, it was all worth it just to know that this guy accepted me. It was all so overwhelming to me but I knew that I would have to make some life changing, difficult choices.

As I grew older and matured, I often asked myself if this guy really, truly felt love or lust for me? Or could it be that I was just another girl to him? Nobody special! Was I thrown into the pool of all the other girls he had been with? Only time would tell. As time went on, I begin to believe in this thing call love. What could a 13 yr. old soon to be 14 year old girl know about love? All I knew for sure is that most of my days were now filled with the WOW factor, moments and feelings of excitement! Finally, the ugly duckling had received her first kiss from the man of her dreams. Imagine the excitement!

Subsequently, during that time, I did not realize that this guy was not the man for me. Besides, I was too young to be talking about love. All I knew, is just that it felt so good.

I lost focus and I could not see beyond this guy's many lies and deception. They say that love is blind. Well it sure is! I say that I was blind to the true character of this guy. I remembered seeing other women on TV fall in love and I knew for certain that my parents were in love but boy I had a lot to learn. For me, the term "boyfriend" sounded amusing, it was like music to my ear and a dream come true. I had finally gotten myself a boyfriend and the last thing on earth that I thought about was pleasing God. If I was planning to keep my boyfriend and cultivate this "boyfriend/girlfriend" relationship then I knew that even more difficult choices and decisions would be forthcoming. I knew that I was brought up in a strict, conservative home and I made choices that were contrary to my Christian upbringing. At the time, Christianity was nowhere in my equation.

In the book of Proverbs 10 verses 1-14 King Solomon's message reveals a contrast between a foolish spirits verses a wise spirit. These scriptures taught me many lessons during my adulthood. These were lessons that I never really understood as a young girl. For these reason, I later learned that *I must always walk in total obedience to the Holy Spirit.* I also realized that *I must follow God's commandments daily.* I understand that if I choose to disobey and live a life of fleshly desires coupled with a lack of intimacy with God, self-indulgence and worldly gain that my outcome would be total destruction and unfruitfulness in my spirit and natural life.

I later realized that my biggest mistake in life was that I failed to consult God first. I didn't consult God prior to making life changing decisions regarding my relationship with this man. Although, this guy would do nice things for me for no charge such as pick me up from school, etc. I never questioned his ulterior motives. I later learned that nothing in life is free! All I can remember is proudly waving goodbye to my friends when he arrived to take me home. Oh, My God, I was in love or so I thought and my parents had no earthly idea of what was going on. They had no idea that this young man was 17 years old, three times my age or so it seemed. But, would my parent's opinion have even mattered at this time?

All I cared about at this point was that I finally found someone that wanted me. The past pain of rejection that I often felt was gradually fading away quickly. This guy and I ended up dating for approximately six plus months before I finally gave in and surrendered myself to him. Giving in would prove to be an inexcusable life altering experience. One of the biggest, sinful, mistakes of my life! Approximately four months later I was with child, pregnant, and that's when his true colors and motives became clear to me. I began to see another side of his character.

He was tainted, untruthful and dishonest. And now I am feeling all alone and confused. His deceitfulness left me broken, naked, and a shame. Then the light is turned on me in to the dark corner in which I tried to hide from my Creator. Shaking before Him seeking repentance and redemption from Him. What will I do? After all I am just a little girl, who has become an unsacred handmaiden of God. And then he did just what any immature childish boy would do…He ran. He was no longer my guy and eventually this so called "one for me" abandoned me for another girl.

So at the age of 14, I found myself very pregnant and all alone with no father to help me care for and raise my unborn baby. Be reminded that I was also attending high school during this time. What would be the fate of my life now? Only God knew the plan for my life. *In Jeremiah 29:11 the Word of God tells me: "For I know the plans I have*

for you, declares the Lord. "Plans to prosper
you and not to harm you, plans to give you
hope and a future. "

 During this time of turmoil in my young
life, I had no other choice except to depend
on God alone with my parents to help me
out of this dilemma. Once my parents found
out about my pregnancy, much pain, sadness
and even feelings of suicide began to plague
my mind. I was so ashamed of myself. I
felt lonesome, foolish and abandoned.
Understandably, one of my parent's primary
concerns was for me to complete my
education. When they realized the
possibility or lack thereof of that actually
happening any time soon, they were even
more disappointed in my decisions.
Negative thoughts soon begin to surface in
my mind as I entertained thoughts that my

life must be ruined now and as time went on so was my reputation. Many of my friend's parents refused to allow them to associate with me. And, to add injury to insult many of the teachers starred at me. I was an "outcast" and people were reluctant in trying to hide their feelings of disapproval toward me. I had an agonizing spirit. I recall walking through the halls of school hearing my fellow classmate's snickers, as others just pointed their fingers in disgust and laughed at me. I asked myself who *Am I and Would I ever become someone with a purpose?*

Eventually I gave birth to my daughter, but things seemingly got worse. I am a teenage mother now. The tasks and obligations such as making baby formula in clean sterile bottles, diaper changings, lack of sleep, baby crying all night, and the arguments and disagreements with my parents was overwhelming. I felt as though I was going crazy. As time went on and I reached my 17th birthday, the increasing pressure to move out of my parents' house became apparent. I was frequently reminded that I would never mean or be anything to anybody or any man. Many people told me that I'd never amount to anything except being labeled as another welfare charity case. Hurray! As God would have it I proved all the naysayers wrong and I finally graduated from high school with my Diploma. With that accomplishment still came disapproval and discord in my parents'. Also another pregnancy approximately two years later. I was pregnant again and so I had no other alternative except to move into my own apartment. The increasing stress of single parenting, grown up responsibilities, paying bills, etc. became overwhelming for me. I honestly think that the visiting roaches and rats probably ate better than me, however, I was determined to succeed and better yet become a survivor. I wanted to prove to all the naysayers including some of my own family members and friends that I could achieve and accomplish a better life for myself and my children.

Without a doubt, it was my children that motivated me to go on. I did not want to fail them. You see, *failing was not an option.* These beautiful young souls depended solely on me for their livelihood. They were worth it all and they were my exclusive reason for striving and surviving!

Let me inspire, motivate, and encourage you to walk with God peacefully. However, to the contrary walking with God is no easy task. Hence, it's no "walk in the park." Walking with God is an enormous commitment of faith, often times it can also be a challenging undertaking. Be encouraged in knowing that you do not have to walk this road alone because God is there with you. All too often, many of us have experienced and can share with others our personal testimonies of the difficulty of walking with God. While walking with God is no skip in the park, it is rewarding and everlasting. Do you recall the time that Moses walked with God through difficult times and adversity? God was with Moses. God is with us. When we take hold of God's unchanging hand and we decide to walk with Him, He will walk with us and He will never leave us alone.

Perhaps, at this time you are wondering why I would ever compare myself to other people. Why compare myself to my family, peers, ministry, marriages, other relationships, and occasionally, even more attractive women? The answer is simple… I was distracted and focused on the wrong things. I was focused on the external rather than the God of my salvation. You see, man looks on the outside, but God looks on the heart. God redirected my attention to Him and I have experienced much intimacy with the Lord as never before. God changed my way of thinking, He changed my heart, mind, and thoughts. The scriptures tell us that God's thoughts are higher than our thoughts and His ways are not our ways.

Therefore, I knew that I had to recondition my mind of those "limited" thoughts. Sadly, my "limited thought process never allowed me to think highly of myself. More importantly, my "limited mindset" never allowed me to focus clearly on the importance of who I was in Christ and the God that created me. You see, I was created in the likeness and image of God. I was created to praise and worship my God! For He is the author and finisher of my faith.

Have you ever taken a moment to just thank God for life and for the freedom to make choices in life? So often, we miss the mark in terms of priorities in life and giving God thanks. We fall short of His glory and we take God's goodness for granted. **Who Am I** to be called worthy of His blessings? **Who Am I** to be deserving of God's own Son?

Who Am I? You have read that as a single mother, I felt so overwhelmed with the everyday normal duties of a mother. That was the consequences of a wrong choice I made. So, as I continue to share with you my thoughts of Who I Am, where I'm going and my journey's woes in getting there... my hope and prayer is that you will better understand through your own pain and sufferings that adverse situations oftentimes come to distract you and to keep you from the promises of God. God's presence in your life will strengthen and propel you to walk faithfully into your divine destiny that God has purposed for your life.

One day I was blessed to meet a wonderful woman. The Lord must have sent her. She befriended me and I could share with her my personal experiences. She was a much older woman but we communicated well. She told me that my parents really loved me and that they were only disappointed in my choices. No one knew the depth of the pain that I experienced. The pain was so deep almost unbearable. By now, I was starting to miss my friends and I missed the fun of participating in other school events. Let me be totally transparent with you because I am a firm believer that the truth will set you free! Every day was not a ray of sunshine, there were moments when I could not see past the pain and I certainly didn't believe that I had a chance for a normal future. She, (My Angel) told me that regardless of my mistakes or I make another now or later, "my goal in life should be to focus on my children and my education".

Chapter 4

Who Am I Becoming?

Therefore if any man be *in Christ,* he is *a new creature: old things are passed away; behold, all things are become new.*
2 Corinthians 5:17

In the book of Proverbs wisdom begins with God. His centrality is assumed throughout. The wise, upright, righteous and godly are equated. They are those who trust and know their God, and mirror this by their just and loving conduct toward their fellows in accordance with their divinely-approved principles. Good and bad are linked with reward and penalty, because God embodies in Himself both love and justice and so must promote good and obviate evil.

The scriptures in the book of Proverbs often refers to the path and the way, indicating conduct and lifestyle and providing both a goal and a means to reach the goal. Our goals can also be perceived as a successful living and the routes to goals is the path of wisdom. I realized that a new beginning for me would involve using wisdom and knowledge. I needed much of both wisdom and knowledge but most importantly I needed the rewards from God through my obedience to Him.

In Proverbs 7:4-5 Says, unto wisdom, Thou art my sister; and call understanding thy kinswoman; that they may keep thee from the strange woman, from the stranger which flatter with her words. I felt the power of the Holy Spirit saying I should embrace wisdom as though I'm embracing a family member that I love and trust deeply. The Holy Spirit is revealing to me the importance of embracing God's wisdom concerning my life. It feels as though a blanket of God's wisdom is connected to my soul much like a mother's connection to her child. As individuals, it's highly important that we understand that God's wisdom is the only divine wisdom that comes directly from the Holy Spirit. I've learned over the years that my relationship with the Lord must be deeper than the depths of the ocean and wider than the sea. It must be far greater than my relationship with people. This new found revelation and though process blessed me during my high school graduation.

Accordingly, I accomplished one of my short term goals and graduated from high school. Although, I didn't graduate with honors, I did, however, graduate with pride and a great sense of accomplishment! I gained greater self-confidence. I was standing on the promises of *Philippians 4:13* ***"I can do all things through Christ which strengthens me."*** At last, I had accomplished my goal but the ride would not end there. The journey has just begun. To my surprise, my teachers, educators, including my family and my parents gave me an unforgettable priceless gift of support and love. That was something that I couldn't buy or get elsewhere.

Have you ever felt an overwhelming degree of love and excitement to the point that you just wanted to rest in it forever? As a result of these brighter days, my spirit was once again lifted. I was in a happy place and despair had no domain in my life. I soon started questioning if I was college material. This notion of college all started to materialize in my mind. All I knew is that the thought of college enrollment sounded good to me. And, to that point, I began to research and explore my options regarding college. **So, Who Am I** - I'm a prospective college student!

I submit to you that we as individuals, created by God, and in the mere image of God, must always desire greater than our intellect can conceive. We must press daily toward the mark for the prize of the high calling of God in Christ Jesus. *Philippians 3:14-15.* We must not cease to believe, achieve and to reach our goals, dreams, visions, and aspirations that the Lord has provided for us.

What an amazing opportunity for me to share before you today to tell you "yes, I did" I successfully completed college and received my bachelor's degree! Yes, I can and yes, I am more than a conqueror through Christ Jesus! I am encouraged as the scriptures minister to my soul. I am, moreover, encouraged to believe in myself and in the power of God working in my life! **Who Am I?** I'm a college graduate.

Romans 8:37 Nay, in all these things, we are more than conquers through Him that love us.

This scripture helps us to understand that we must press our way in order to receive what God has for us. Occasionally, there will be times in your life when you may feel defeated and just want to give up on life due to the overwhelming trials, and challenges that may be beyond your control. These are the roller coaster emotions that I have often felt during my journey. However, I have decided to press my way through! I have decided to press my way while being a single parent! I have decided to press my way while pursuing a higher education! I have decided to press my way as a professional leader! I have decided to press my way as a wife, as a teacher and as a Minister of the Gospel of Jesus Christ!

I want to encourage you to press on even when you are faced with challenges in life. Press your way through and believe that with God all things are possible to those that believes. **Who Am I?** I'm a conqueror through Christ Jesus!

In Revelation 14:12, we are encouraged to endure every trial and persecution, for we are His saints who remain firm to the end in obedience to His commands and trust in Jesus." As a final note and a reflection of my life's experiences, I have come to an understanding that the person that I once was cannot be defined by the woman of God that I have become! In other words, my past does not define my future!

Chapter 5

The Un-Named, Missing Faces

He forgives all my sins and
heals all my diseases
Psalm 103:3 NLT

This chapter in my book is extremely
personal, painful, purposeful and powerful
for me to discuss. However, I pray that my
transparency will bless thousands of women
that may be contemplating ending a
pregnancy or perhaps, may have previously
prematurely ended a pregnancy and or given
up children for personal reasons. May I
remind you that I am not a perfect individual
and neither are any humans on this earth?
For that reason alone, I have definitely made
my share of mistakes alone the way, ***but for
the Grace of God!*** God's grace has been

sufficient for me and His love has covered a multitude of my sins.

Obviously, by now it is evident by the title of this chapter that I have made some dreadful mistakes in my past. Previously, I shared with you in detail my relationship with this older man and how I fell in love with him at the age of 14. In addition, I also shared with you my first pregnancy which resulted in the birth of my oldest daughter. Frankly, there were other pregnancies that some of you may or may not be aware of. While my past decisions lacked judgement and wisdom, I am convinced, after asking my Lord and Savior to forgive me, that I am forgiven. *"For I will be merciful to their unrighteousness, and their sins and their iniquities will I remember no more." Hebrews 8:12.*

As a young woman, teenager or an adult you may experience an unwanted pregnancy due to circumstances in your life. Who's to blame when misfortunes or difficult decisions come your way? Ask yourself am I the reason? Were there other people involved? Did I seek the Lord first or the Holy Spirit for guidance regarding this dilemma in my life? I have had many sleepless nights due to tormenting dreams from horrible choices that I had to make regarding my unnamed children. My choices today would certainly be different. But doing the 70's 80's and 90's we were led by the medical opinions that it was a safe method of birth control. My total uneducated ignorance of terminating a pregnancy made me a part of a vile statistics.

As a young woman with much baggage of despair, hopelessness and uncertainties in many of my relationships, I felt in my heart that I was making the right decision at the time. My heart had been broken for many years, and I've carried some deep rooted issues that have never been addressed concerning my unnamed children. When the different pregnancies occurred there were many mixed emotions and questions in regards to **Who Am I** regarding God's child? Who Am I and What Will People Think of Me? How many of you have experienced this or similar reoccurring thoughts in your own mind because you too may have made the wrong decision?

The fathers of our unnamed children's never stood up to be accountable for those treacherous acts, they were not the real men I needed them to be. In fact, they never even acknowledged or expressed any love, or concern for me or our un-named sons or daughters, the babies. Perhaps, *unspoken* words speak louder than actual words.

When I think about that pivotal turning points in my life, I'm sure this was by far one of the hardest things that I've ever had to endure. I believed in my heart, without a shadow of a doubt, that these past experiences and poor choices are the driving force behind my profound and unconditional love that draws me so much closer to my living children. Each and every one of them lives in the closet of my heart.

For many years I avoided sharing these very personal and intimate details with anyone including my five living children due to fear, shame, hurt and the guilt that accompany my past decisions. As such, I believe in my heart and I am confident that a divine healing is taking place for countless women all over this Universe. I believe that God has called me to share my story for such a time as this. I give total praise, honor, and glory to God for giving me the courage, strength and determination to be completely open, honest and transparent with you. My ultimate goal and sincere prayer is that my story will enlighten you and discourage others from making the same or similar mistakes that I have experienced.

While these poor choices have resulted in emotional pain for me, they have also adversely impacted me physically. Above all, I am extremely grateful and blessed to be able to share my experiences. I want to encourage you to not give up, don't give in and don't give out! Rest assured that that God will not give up on you!

In retrospect, our trials only come to make us strong. During our times of weakness, God's strength is made perfect. Therefore beloved, find your strength in God! Trust Him for your healing and deliverance!

While I have suffered much, yet, I reign with Christ! I thank God daily for His unconditional love toward me. He looked beyond my faults and saw my needs. He sees the innermost, deepest parts of my heart yet He loves me the same! He loves me in spite of my poor prior decisions and there is absolutely nothing in this world that will ever change God's love toward me. How comforting to have that assurance of God's love. Likewise, God loves you in spite of all the things that you've ever done wrong. God loves you with an Agape love (unconditional love) and God is able to turn all of your wrongs into rights. What a Mighty good God we serve! Angels bow before Him, Heaven and Earth adores Him. What a Mighty God we serve! Trust God and allow Him to direct your paths. The Lord has given me his love unconditionally, without prerequisites and I'm so grateful. My five beautiful children Kimberly, Telia, Mia, Tiffany and Tyrone have been the heartbeats of my life since the age 14 ½ and I'm so grateful to God for them. I thank God for them daily. I love them more than life itself!

WHO AM I? I'm a loving mother to four beautiful girls and the most handsome son in my universe.

Front row: Kimberly   Center row: Mia, Pastor Debbie, Tiffany   Back row: Tyrone, Telia

And he said unto me, my grace is sufficient for thee; for my strength is made perfect in weakness. 2 Corinthians 12:9

God has given me grace in the lives of my five beautiful Son and Daughters.

Chapter 6

The Wings beneath My Feet

And He rode on a cherub and flew; And He appeared
on the wings of the wind
2 Samuel 22:11

When I think of the word <u>SISTER</u> I immediately think of a loving female that shares a special bond with other siblings. What are some of the thoughts that comes to your mind when you hear the word Sister. Is there a specific person or individuals that come to your mind? During my research of the word sister, the dictionary defines sister as… **A woman or girl in relation to other daughters and/or sons of her parents.** During my lifetime, there has been many women of color that fits that profile.

Interestingly, these women have been enormously influential, loving, kind and supportive toward me. Specifically, there are three very special women that appropriately fit that profile to a T. There is no question in my mind that these women were sent by God. They have exemplified faith, love, support and encouragement toward me during my graduate and undergraduate studies. For these reason, I say "thank you" sisters! Your acts of kindness and compassion toward me will never be forgotten. I pray that you all will receive a double, triple, and even a hundred fold blessing in return for your acts of kindness.

Sisters, you all thought it not strange to embrace me as your very own sister. You all are what I describe as *"Unspoken Heroes,"* you're truly *"The Wings Beneath my*

Feet"! You all have motivated, inspired, and encouraged me to go on even when I didn't feel like going on.

Honestly, I've always had a dream to enroll in college and pursue my Master's Degree. In spite of this, I've always walked the pathway of disbelief regarding this dream. As I reflect back on my journey as I finally achieved my dream, I recall many sleepless nights of lying in bed praying and crying out to God to just please send me someone that wouldn't judge me due to my lack of knowledge and understanding. Notably, I suffered from extreme low self-esteem in regards to my writing abilities and lack of understanding of modern technology. I asked God to send me someone that would understand me and not perceive my questions or lack of knowledge as ignorant, stupid, or just plain old simple minded.

Of course, these were the vivid descriptions in which I viewed myself at that time due to my numerous insecurities in my own talents and abilities. However, since that time, I have learned to embrace my gifts and stand on the promises of *Philippians 4:13 "I can do all things through Christ that strengthens me!"* *Lastly, I would like to express a special thank you to Sharon, Laura, and Amanda for all the hard work, love, support, and encouragement that you all have shown me. Thank you all for not giving up on me when times seemed difficult!* *You are my SISTERS*

Ironically, I have meet many women (young and old) pursuing their God given dreams and goals of completing their college education and obtaining their graduate level degrees from various universities. I distinctly recall wishing that I could be one of those women. Just imagine little Debbie in college, not to mention Grad school! What an amazing blessing and an awesome accomplishment! Could that really be the path that God was leading me to? I recall a specific prayer one day in my prayer closet. I remember asking God "Lord I need for you to please send me someone to help me complete my education. Someone who would recognize my value and see my self-worth. Someone who would help me overcome my fears of failure. Someone who had faith and who believed in me. Someone that would be led by the Holy Spirit. I also discussed with the Lord my past hurts, disappointments, and embarrassments. These things plagued my spirit for many years and prevented me from pursuing my college education. Of course, God knew all about what I was going through even before I uttered the words from my mouth. It is with great pleasure and a humble heart that I submit to you today that GOD DID IT! Yes, God did it for me and I enrolled in college and graduate school and obtained both my Bachelor and Master degrees! ***Praise The Lord! To God Be the Glory!!!***

Once again, I would find myself asking the Lord the exact same question as before "Lord, Who Am I today?" I Am a wife, mom, grandmother, daughter, friend, professional, and a Pastor today? I've always counted it an honor and a privilege to be entrusted with the many roles that God had bestowed upon me. I am eternally grateful and I especially respect the role of serving as a helpmate, lover, supporter and best friend to my husband, Pastor Collin Staples. *"Whoso findeth a wife findeth a good thing, and obtaineth favour of the Lord."*

Proverbs 18:22

In regards to my role as a mom, and grandmother, that job, too, requires the spirit of understanding, love, support, kindness and compassion, all of which I feel that the Lord has blessed me to acquire. In terms of my professional role as an educator, that, too, is demanding and requires patience. However, God has been faithful to equip me with the academic tools, and I have learned the traits of the profession. In short, I have gained a better understanding of ethics in leadership, respect, value, and support for others just to name a few.

Nevertheless, through it all, my role as a Co-Pastor has been one of the most rewarding assignments entrusted to me. Specifically, this platform has blessed me relentlessly with the opportunity to be a blessing to others and to be used by God as His very own mouth piece. As such, I am honored to be anointed and called by God to preach salvation to the captives and to share with His people the truth of the Gospel of Jesus Christ! One thing that I know for sure is that the Lord will grant us blessings and supernatural favor if we keep our minds stayed on Him. We must live a life that is pleasing in His sight. We must abandon our ways and submit to His will and His way for our lives. Most importantly, we must learn to lean not unto our own understanding, but in all our ways acknowledge Him and He will direct our path.

Another important truth I've learned after reading the book of Proverbs Chapter 12, is that a mind of unrighteousness and wicked behavior resulted in King Solomon defeat and a life of sin against God. As you continue to read this book, I encourage you to resist sin, do not allow sin to manifest and take root in your life. Keep your heart and mind stayed on God and He will take care of you.

The notion that total pleasure comes from a sinful lifestyle is farthest from the truth. Let me enlighten you, the truth of the matter is that a sinful lifestyle will only provide temporary pleasures. To the contrary, a Holy and righteous lifestyle results in eternal life! Remember, when God is the center of your life, the deeds of wickedness will no longer have dominion over your life.

More often than not, the demanding expectations of society can cause you to believe that you must be or become everything that others desire you to be. That's simply not true. You should strive to be what God has called you to be.

As I continue to pray to the Lord, I hear an inner voice from the Holy Spirit speaking softly to my soul. *"Debbie, I've set you free from the pain, burden, regrets and despair of not meeting everyone's expectations."* God has set my soul free and the scripture reminds us that those who the Son sets free are free indeed! *Who Am I? I am Free!*

These words truly liberated and empowered me to continue becoming the woman that

God has called me to be. Sometimes we have to discover within ourselves, exactly what's our true identity in God? Could it be that your true identity is being withheld and hidden in secret places? Your secret place may be an illusions of your mind, or in the captivity of your soul.

The identity of who you are and who you're becoming is essential to your purpose and destiny in life.

In the past I've hidden myself because of the shame and guilt of my past. The shame had once paved my heart with so much guilt and sadness. There were pavements and pavements of constructed concrete layers such as "What if this had happened and what if that had happened? What if I had listened to my parents? Should I have given up my virginity at such a young age? Should I have married at such a young age? Should I have given birth to all my children? Should I have left my home state? And should I have stayed in an abusive marriage?"

Obviously, my inner emotions were becoming filled with the expectations of people rather than the expectations of God, my Lord and Savior. Let me warn you that there will be times in your life when you must ask yourself Who **Am I** and exactly **who am I living for**? Am I living for people or God? People would have you to think that you are obligated to them, however, I am discovering every day that I am living for God. I am God's beloved daughter. I have a past, I have a present, and my future lies in His hands! I was created for God's glory and I am becoming what God has ordained for my life.

Who Am I*? I'm a child of the Most High God! I'm Pastor Debbie Staples!*

Chapter 7

A Woman with a Prophetic Purpose

*The Spirit of the Lord is upon me, because
he hath anointed me to preach the gospel to
the poor; he hath sent me to heal the
brokenhearted, to preach deliverance to the
captives, and recovering of sight to the
blind, to set at liberty them that are
bruised,
To preach the acceptable year of the Lord
Luke 4: 18-19*

In this Chapter I will share with you my
most intimate devotional times with God
and the Holy Spirit. To be quite honest with
you, I must admit that there were many
times in my life that I would never have
imagined or even believed that God could
use someone like me for His Glory. When I
reflect back over my life including the good,

bad, and the ugliness, I realize that I am blessed! I am better than blessed. Praise the Lord! And while the enemy would have both me and you to believe that we are unworthy and undeserving of God's own Son and God's unconditional love, *the devil is a liar*!

Jesus gave up His life and died on the Cross for my sins, for your sins and for the sins of the world so that we might have the right to the tree of life. Jesus became sin so that we may become the righteousness of God through Christ Jesus! Yes, Jesus died for the salvation of mankind. Therefore, the question becomes, how do I repay Him for all that He has done for me? I will give Him my life for the rest of my entire life.

Yes, I accept Jesus as Lord and Savior of my life! Have you accepted Christ as your Lord

and Savior? If not, why not do so today? Just repeat this prayer: "**Dear _Lord, I am a sinner, I confess my sins. I believe that Jesus died on the Cross for my sins. I repent of my sins and I invite you to come into my life and save me."_**
Congratulations! I believe that you have been saved!

God loves you and I discovered many years ago as I was reflecting back over my journal entries that God loves me too! I find solace in knowing that these documented journals expressing my inner thoughts are what actually propelled me to keep the faith in God. I began to love God even more. I realized that God loved me first even when I didn't feel that I deserved to be loved; even when I didn't particularly love myself.

As years passed and I began to mature into the woman that God has ordained for my life, I was presented with an opportunity to speak at a Women's Conference in my home state of Ohio. I can truly tell you that God demonstrated His strength and power as He spoke through me. You see, the natural me struggled internally with what to say to so many women from all walks of life. I wondered what the women were really thinking about me as I was being transparent regarding my life's struggles, challenges and disappointments. Perhaps, I'll never know their exact thoughts, however, one thing that I know for sure is that I was *LIBERATED*!

For the first time in my life, I felt free from the shame, hurt, disappointments and struggles that had once held me bound. These strong holds of the enemy no longer had power over me and as you continue to read this book, my hope and prayer for you is that you, too, will feel a sense of freedom, liberation, boldness, fearlessness, and transparency. I pray that you will be healed and learn to forgive others including yourself for your past mistakes and shortcomings. Finally, I pray that you will walk into your destiny of greatness that God has ordained for you!

Initially, when I was asked to speak at the conference, I began to question myself and my abilities. I consulted with the Lord by asking Him to tell me what I could possibly have to share with so many wonderful women. I recall telling the Lord that I was nothing and nobody and furthermore, my life was so unworthy of sharing with others. I thought, at the time, that I did not have a prophetic purpose on my life. I felt that I didn't have a destiny or ever embarked on a journey of substance.

I told the Lord, "My Lord, never in a million years could I have imagined myself fulfilling a purpose for you." But, as I began to stand before the women at the conference, I noticed that I had captured their undivided attention and their eyes were all filled with tears. The tissue boxes were being passed around the room to and fro, and the sad spirit that once consumed the room when I initially stated to the women that I felt that I was nothing! Suddenly a change overtook the room and the atmosphere was filled with the Shekinah glory ushering in the Spirit of the Lord; as the Holy Spirt moved mightily within my soul, spirit, and throughout the room. My heart continued beating rapidly and my voice became unrecognizable in the natural as I struggled revealing my past.

I began to say "Lord I'm nothing!" I reiterated, "I'm nothing!" I'm nothing so how is it possible for you to use me and my story to help heal these women of much brokenness? I could clearly hear the Holy Spirit speaking to me telling me to "Be transparent and I'll do the rest, my daughter."

The Bible story about the Samarian Woman immediately came to my mind and this was the pivotal point of my deliverance and healing. This Samarian woman seemed to pull strongly at my inner soul. This woman's story related to my past relationships with my children's fathers. In John Chapter 4, the author tells us about a Samarian woman and her relationships with different men. This story resonated deeply in my spirit as I began to think about my past and present relationships, and the heartaches that I have had to endure. I found myself standing there trembling as though I couldn't speak a word. The Samarian woman had many relationships much like myself. However, she and I had something profoundly divine in common. We both had a thirst for a deeper and more intimate relationship with God. As I was sharing my story with the women at the conference, a particular scripture in John came to mind: ***John 4:13 "But whosoever drinketh of the water that I shall give him shall never thirst; but the water that I shall give him shall be in him a well of water springing up into everlasting life."***

In the past, this passage of scripture had often perplexed me. I question why the woman was even at the well on the sixth hour of the day. Historically, the sixth hour of the day is usually the hottest hour of the day. Still, no one else was there at the well except for Jesus and the woman. The Holy Spirit spoke to me and instructed me to ask the women attending the conference to visualize themselves standing in front of the well and suddenly notice Jesus walking up as He starts to reveal to them everything about their life from beginning to end. I asked them to imagine themselves being at the well with a desire to be alone so that no one would find out and judge them for their past mistakes. I, too, imagined myself standing at a well in my spirit thinking about my pregnancy at the age of 14 and feeling un-forgiveness, and I reiterate that I didn't see myself as a woman with a prophetic purpose. At that particular time in my life no one could see or even think of me as a woman of purpose. The only thing that people could see in me was my past mistakes and failures. *Thank God that He looked beyond my faults and saw my need!*

"Who Are You?" Was the exact question that I inquired of the women at the conference? I shared my story with them; I told them that at the age of 14 I was pregnant and by the age of 18 I was graduating from high school with another baby on the way. There were two different fathers and by the age of 20 I was married to a man who was an alcoholic and constantly used me as his punching bag due to his addiction. So where were my friends and where was God? I felt all alone but later in life I realized that God was always there with me. He's the reason why I am still alive today and able to share my story.

There was particular season in my life, when I was ill a majority of the time. I experienced feelings of stress and anxiety coupled with fear and shame. I noticed that whenever I decided to open the door to my natural home and heart, people would recognize my brokenness, they would see the black eyes, and the swollen face from the physical abuse and assaults from the hands of my so-called husband at the time. I remember that most days, during my first marriage, were horrible days. I was hungry most of the time due to a lack of money to buy food and pay bills. Time after time, I would ask myself "what is my purpose in life and why was I even living?" What could it possibly be that the Lord would have me to be or experience in this life? I began to feel like Job in the Bible with so many horrific tragedies happening, my faith in God remained steadfast.

As I continued to embrace this thing called life, I recall constantly moving from one apartment to another. I experienced evictions, I became pregnant with another child in addition to experiencing more sickness, sexually transmitted diseases, hospitalization, more abuse, financial hardship, homelessness, and the list goes on.

My relationship with daily turmoil was evident. I begin to ask myself again and again what my purpose for living was. It seemed as though this season in my life consisted of parallel twists, and turns, unrealistic, unbelievable misfortunes and so many expectations from people. I noticed that after I shared my personal challenges with the women at the conference, they all seemed to empathize with my story as they sat there quietly listening as though they had experienced the same or similar treatment.

While I'm on this journey to discover why God has kept me here, I have often wondered if my identity will continue to be hidden in the secret places of my heart. There were still pavements of emotional and physical pain constructed brick by brick, stone by stone that couldn't be broken. I realized that I too, shared many of the same condemnations as the Samarian woman at the well.

I can truly tell you that these were incredibly difficult times in my life and I felt so all alone. It was only later in life that I began to understand that God had never left my side, He was always there with me in the good and most difficult times in my life. While, I openly admit to you that I had experienced much abuse during my first marriage, I assure you that God had a purpose and a plan for my life. All I knew then is that I was on welfare, receiving food stamps, living in roach and mice infected housing with my utilities constantly being disconnected due to nonpayment. In all these hardship, I refused to tell anyone including my immediate family about my situation due to shame and embarrassment. But through it all, ***God had a Prophetic Purpose for my life*** and now I understand that I had to go this route of my journey in order to receive the blessings that God had in store for me.

But when it pleased God, who separated
me from my mother's womb, and called me
by His grace. To reveal His Son in me, that
I might preach Him among the heathen;
immediately I conferred not with
flesh and blood. Galatians 1:15-16

Chapter 8

My Soul Mate

Whoso findeth a wife findeth a good thing,
and obtaineth favour of the LORD
                                        Proverbs 18:22

As years passed and two divorces later.
And, after losing my financial stability, my
confidence in finding true love, my home to
foreclosure, and losing so many other things
in life, I realized that I am enormously
blessed to have been able to survive it all
and complete my degree in Early Childhood
Education. As such, my life began to unfold
in a more positive direction. I began to walk
with baby steps in pursuit of my purpose and
God's plan for my life. In spite of being
viewed as a discarded spoil due to my
mistakes, misfortunes, and challenges, the
Lord saw fit to bless me with the love of my

life, my current husband, and my soul mate of 21 years, Pastor Collin Staples. Our courtship began on a Saturday morning when I was taking my son for his weekly haircut. I arrived at the barbershop for my son's haircut appointment. As soon as I was on my way out the door, I paused quickly in order to make a phone call at the phone booth. For my younger readers, phone booths were the common means of communication prior to the cell phone existence. I distinctly recall attempting to make the call, however, I discovered that I needed change and as I begin searching in my purse for 25 cents, the cost of a phone call during that time, I recall a gentleman asking me if I needed help.

I couldn't believe the audacity of this man standing behind me asking me if I needed help. I suddenly turned around and low and behold there stood a man with the most beautiful smile I've ever seen in my life! As he spoke all I could see was his beautiful white teeth and a sweet humble spirit! We talked and he eventually gave me a quarter to make my phone call. Strangely, he continued to stand there as though he was lost. After a few minutes he asked me my name and he told me that he would love to call me sometimes. Little did he know, I was not interested in him or any other man. I was going through an awful divorce, five children, one grandbaby, working two jobs, attending college, and my attitude toward men was extremely bad, and rightfully so!

I must honestly admit that this gentleman was very sweet and respectful toward me. This was something that I had not experienced in the past. However, there were still one key problem, this just wasn't the right time for me. I had too much going on in my life. I had too much baggage and the last thing that I was thinking about was another relationship. I was determined not to get involved with another man due to the hurt, pain, suffering, rejection and low self-esteem that I was experiencing in my mind, soul and spirit. Unfortunately, I decided to give this young man the wrong phone number. In exchange, he gave me his correct phone number. After we said our good-byes at the barbershop, I returned home. His phone number was thrown in the top drawer of mess in my bedroom. Coincidently, after about two to three months of trying to figure out my life and what I should be doing in terms of my future, I finally broke down and called this guy. That decision has proven to be one of the best decisions that I've ever made in my life! To this day, I have no regrets!!!

Now, a very bizarre thing happened prior to me calling this man. I actually had a dream about him and I recall waking up that Sunday morning searching for his number. This all started around 7:00 a.m. in the morning and I couldn't believe the desperation to find this guy's number. Interestingly, I couldn't even remember his name, but I remembered his kindness. Finally, I found the paper with his number written on it and I called him that Sunday morning. I'll never forget that moment because when he answered the phone he was so surprised to hear from me. His first question was, why did you give me the wrong phone number? I had many reasons for doing so but I didn't share them all. Finally he asked me... what are you doing today? My reply was nothing! So he asked me...would you like to join me at Church today? My first response was...are you kidding me? You can't be serious! Surely he must have a girlfriend I thought. The questions ran rapidly in my mind but eventually I said yes! I would love to attend Church with you.

After that initial Church date, we ended up dating for about five or six months before he asked me to marry him. He promised me that he would take care of me, my five children, and my grandbaby for the rest of his life. I thought that this all sounded unreal, too good to be true, but look at God once again giving me what He felt that I needed here on this Earth. Yes! I said, Yes!

Now, who would have ever imagined a man wanting to marry a woman with so much baggage? A woman of rejection, insecurities, low self-esteem, five children, a grandbaby, financial issues, divorced, and so on. God was truly in the beginning of this relationship, He's still in the midst of our marriage and God will be with us for eternity! God definitely had a plan that I didn't understand!

After a few months, Collin and I were soon married and it has been a journey of a lifetime with its many twists and turns. Twists, tunnels, curves, straight ways, love, misunderstandings, love, disagreements, love, and sometimes bitterness. Everyday has not been a bed of roses. We've had our ups and downs. We have needed God more than we have needed anything or anyone else. We've needed God more than we have needed food to sustain our health, body, mind and soul. Our marriage consisted of a blended family with nine children, and a combined 25 grandchildren that we love with all of our hearts!

I can tell you that we've experienced good times and not so good times. Specifically, we've experienced unimaginable sad times in our life as we have had to bury two of our grandsons. These times are what brings us closer as a family. Their death was devastating on our family and it nearly caused me an emotional breakdown. I can honestly say that the Lord alone with my amazing husband have been there for me through it all. I have been healed and

delivered from sorrow and sadness.
Although our marriage has gone through the
fire, it honestly survived by the power and
grace of our Lord and Savior Jesus Christ.
Do we have challenges? Yes we do! Have
we discussed throwing in the towel? Yes we
have! Do our children have issues? Yes they
do! However, we have learned over the
years how to trust the Lord through it all
even when things seem too impossible for
man.

Our spiritual walk with God has given us the
spiritual tools, a foundation, guidelines, and
the blue print to keep our marriage together
before our Lord and Savior.

While some couples have given up on each
other and their marriage, we are fully aware
that there are many marriages that have
endured the storm and haven't seen a

resolve. But we choose to make our marriage work! We chose eternity in God!

You see, a good marriage will always cost something in terms of sacrifice, commitment, love, faith, patience, endurance, communication, and trust just to name a few. Most importantly, we've learned how to trust God when times get rough and the storms of life are raging. We've learned that our relationship is worth too much to just give up on it and throw in the towel. God has invested His spirit into this marriage and set us as a spectacle before all that would see how the constant building of His kingdom will look with His sanctified husband and wife. We understand that our relationship is not only a commitment to each other but also a commitment to God.

For better, for worse, for richer and for poor! And For His Church...

We have learned to trust the Lord to bring us through whatever difficulties that we may be facing. Who Am I to determine my fate? Who Am I to decide what's best for me? *I'm a beloved daughter of the Most High God!* Only God knows what's best for me and my life. *Only God knows what's best for our marriage.* *I thank God for the 21 years with my husband Pastor Collin Staples!* I will continue to bless the Lord and give Him glory during this season in my life. As Christian women, we must understand that God has given us our husbands so that we can be their helpmates, and soulmates.

I encourage each of you to continue to seek the Holy Spirit to lead and direct you in your marriage!

Pastors Collin & Debbie Staples

For I know the thoughts I think toward you', says the Lord, thoughts of peace and not of evil, to give you an expected end. Jeremiah 29:11 KJV

Who I Am?

Mother

Wife

Daughter

Christian

Servant

Grandmother

Woman of God

Minister of the Gospel of
Jesus Christ

Teacher

Dreamer

Helpmate

Disciple for Christ

Woman of Purpose

Peace Keeper

WHO ARE YOU?

Use the Space Below to
Describe Who You Are!

_____

_____

_____

_____

_____

_____

_____

_____

_____

_____

_____

_____

_____

_____

Bibliography

Unless otherwise identified, KJV Scripture quotations are from

the King James Version of the Bible.

LBTV is scripture taken from the Living Bible Translation Version
Copyright © 2011. Used by permission. All rights reserved.

NLT is scripture taken from the New Living Translation Version of the Bible.
Copyright© 25 Oct 2012. Used by permission. All rights reserved.

ESV is scripture taken from the English Standard Version. Bible Gateway. Web.
Copyright© 25 Oct 2012. Used by permission. All rights reserved.

About the Author

Who Am I?

Debbie Staples... born April 22, 1961 she is the Pastor of Naked and Not Ashamed Ministries, where she pastors with her husband Pastor Collin Staples. Pastor Debbie received her Bachelors of Science degree in the field of Education from Otterbein College in Westerville, Ohio. And a Master's Degree from Marygrove College She is currently an educator for Columbus City Schools in Columbus, Ohio. Pastor Debbie Staples and her husband Pastor Collin Staples are the parents of five children and 25 grandchildren.

Pastor Debbie believes with the Lord you can do all things but fail. I present myself before you with a humble heart, a loving spirit, and an unconditional love for all God's people and His children; my greatest desire is to have a heart like my Lord and Savior, to love, show kindness, acceptance and compassion for all individuals in every walk of life.

For Book Signings

Speaking Engagements

For additional copies of this book

Contact: Author, Debbie Staples

e-mail: dcla.sstaples@aol.com
https.//whoamidstaples.wixsite.com